Copyright Notice

First Printing, 2012
ISBN-13: 978-1478144106
ISBN-10: 1478144106

Printed in the United States of America

Table of Contents

Introduction

Thank you for picking up your copy of Direct Day Game Method by me Charlie Valentino.

Why do I practice direct day game and only direct day game? The answer is simple! In fact that is the answer; it is the simplest method of pick up there is.

Like many people new to pick up, I once suffered from extreme approach anxiety. This was partly because I was following other people's methods that were not right for me.

True, direct day game (DDG) may not be the one method that is right for you, there are many ways of meeting women and many approaches and styles you can use. However it is DDG that has proven to be by far the best method at least for me and is the one method I'm going to teach you in this book.

It is my hope that after reading this book, you'll find approaching women in the street, coffee shop or shopping mall easy.

Feel free to disagree with me at any point in this book, I am only giving you my opinion and telling you what I know works best for me. Having said that, I strongly believe that DDG should be the method all newbie pick up artists should begin with. I am strongly convinced about the truth of that statement because those starting out really do require the most simple pick up strategy there is, one that does not laden the head down with too many techniques, tactics, routines, games and stories etc. DDG works so well because it is just you and her in the moment with no crap flying around your head. Newbies, many of whom will be suffering from approach anxiety like I did, will really benefit from the simple DDG method for those reasons.

So let's begin on our journey of discovering the easiest and perhaps most effective pick up strategy there is.

Day Game versus Night Game

There are many reasons why I prefer to approach women during the day over approaching them at night in bars, pubs or night clubs.

I know many people who only have the balls to approach women during the night whilst under the influence of alcohol. What does this say about the guy? It says that if he wasn't drunk then he wouldn't be speaking to her. Women can sense this and they really can tell if a man only has the guts to speak to them because he's intoxicated. This is why they use what has become known as the "shit test."

No, during the day you get the real girl and not some act or persona she's putting on while she's out with her friends. And trust me, many girls put this act on, they have to do it because they get hit on all the time. This is even worse for the more attractive girls, they get hit on the most so they have to use some sort of a self-defence mechanism to ward off all the "lower value" guys.

This self-defence mechanism is what we call the "shit test." Have you ever approached a hot girl in a bar, started speaking to her and received nothing back other than the cold shoulder? Perhaps she scrunched her face up at you, turned her back on you or ignored you completely? This is her self defence mechanism at work. If she didn't do this then she'd have so many guys talking to her all night long that she'd never get to spend any time with her friends.

When in this situation, most guys, perhaps 95% will walk away indignantly and tell their mates that she was a bitch. The remaining 5% will show their worth, stick around and show that they are not intimidated. If they are persistent then more often than not they should be able to get into a conversation with her.

However, those few guys, an even smaller percentage than 5%, something like 0.5% who have the balls to approach women in the street, in broad day light without the effects of alcohol running through their system do not have to put up with any of that rubbish such as "shit tests." Out in the street, in the real world during the day, you get the real person, the real girl and you can just skip through all that crap and get straight to the point. That point is this: You saw her and you like her and you want her phone number! It's as simple as that! I like day game because it really is that simple!

During the night, you also have to contend with her group of friends. Sure if you've read other pick up manuals, you'll know all about using your friends to take care of her friends while you speak to your target. But how good at speaking to women are your friends? Can they distract them for long enough for you to get to know your girl? And at any time her friends can get fed up with your friends and pull her friend away from you. This happens a lot! However, during the day time women are most often out by themselves so you don't have to worry about any of this. And if you do see a girl you like the look of who is with a friend then trust me, you won't have much of a problem with her pulling her friend away because this isn't human nature; it's just not polite is it!

During the night, you also have to contend with perhaps a hundred other guys in the bar who all want her phone number. Do you really just want to be another one of those hundred guys? And then what happens if you actually get her number? Will she actually remember giving you it the next day? Most pick up artists (PUA's) agree that phone numbers received at night tend to have high flake rates for this reason.

During the day, you will be the only guy with the balls to approach her so there is literally no competition for you! There's definitely not another hundred guys to contend with so guess what? She'll remember you! You will be the only guy that week, month or perhaps even year who actually had the guts to approach her as she walked up Main Street carrying her shopping. Believe me, this will make you stand out in a huge way!

As I said before, when you speak to girls at clubs and bars, you are more often than not getting an act and not the real person. After all, don't you put on a bit of an act yourself when you're out? You dress differently, walk differently and most probably act a little differently. Well it's the same for her too! During the day, without the influence of alcohol you really are getting the real person, and if she's a bitch then you really are better off without her. You are much more likely to meet a better quality of person, definitely the relationship kind of a girl in a coffee shop than you are in a bar. Besides, girls much prefer telling their friends they met somebody in the coffee shop than in a bar, it just sounds so much nicer.

Yes, I'll state that again; during the day you are more likely to meet the relationship type of girl. If that's what you're after then that's perfect. This book will be great for you if you follow it.

Direct versus Indirect

For a long time it was the indirect method that was preferred amongst the PUA "gurus" however I think that most of them are coming around to the direct method of approaching women.

For those who don't know the difference I will clarify the difference now. Indirect is where you approach a girl going under the radar. You would start by asking her a question, for the time, directions or for her opinion on something. For example, you could ask the girl you see in Starbucks what is the nicer drink out of a mocha or a latte because you're new to Starbucks and you don't have much of an idea what is what. She would then tell you what she prefers. You would then try and elaborate on her response, which you don't really care about anyway because of course you know what a latte is really. So you would end up talking about lattes for a couple of minutes all the while you're trying to find something on her that stands out, something to compliment her on; perhaps she is wearing a distinctive piece of clothing, jewellery or maybe even that you've read the book she's reading. The aim is to try and take the conversation away from lattes and onto something more personal so you can move the pick up attempt along. So you've complimented her on her bracelet and also mentioned your sister has a similar bracelet. Cool! Now would be a suitable time to introduce yourselves and shake hands. Now the next part is the most important part of the entire indirect pick up because you are suddenly shifting into a different mode. You are no longer talking about lattes and are now trying to become acquainted. From any point ahead she may well be expected to slip the word "boyfriend" into the conversation to inform you she has one. So how much time have you wasted up until this point? Five minutes perhaps to find out she has a boyfriend! But let's assume she is single and the pick up continues. You now have to subtly qualify yourself to her to show that you're worth her time and to try and win her over. You have to do this because you didn't go direct, which is in itself all the qualification you need to do to show your worth. So you end up having to tell a few stories about some cool adventures you've taken with your mates to try and impress her. Perhaps you've just come back from travelling or you went skydiving last week; hopefully she'll be impressed. So now let's hope she's opening up a little bit and telling you something about her. You now have to try and get her to qualify to you! So you are asking her qualification questions such as "tell me three things about yourself that will impress me!" At least you'll use that line if you've been reading the material. So now you have to be impressed by what she tells you. By now it's probably dawning on her that this is a pick up attempt, but in reality she probably guessed earlier. Now you have to try and find out some common ground, some reason to see each other again in a more social setting. If you're good at indirect pick up then you will have asked a qualification question that would have given you this information and now you'll be fully aware that you're both interested in going to the movies. From now on getting a phone number should be simple! Just ask for it!

The long paragraph above is a very basic model of an indirect pick up. Of course you can throw in other things as well to make things more complicated such as kino escalation (always a good idea), routines, jokes, games, NLP, cold reads etc.

Also, in a lot of instances indirect approaches such as opinion openers just make no sense at all and you'll find yourself in a very short conversation with a very perplexed girl. It's just not very easy to walk up to a girl in a shopping mall and start talking about what films are good to see at the moment, or what present you should buy for your friend, or what is better a latte or Americano.

Finally, when you take the indirect approach, you're concealing your true intentions to the girl. You're interested in her romantically yet here you are talking about lattes, films or presents. I for one have never been able to pull it off, I just can't be false, I'm a very up front person!

So why not just go direct?

The direct approach is so much more simple and straightforward. The essence of the direct approach is that you see her, you march up to her and you tell her you think she's gorgeous!

The very fact you had the balls to walk up to her during the day and tell her you think she's gorgeous is all the qualification you actually need. So because of this you can actually skip a huge chunk of the usual pick up routine. This streamlined approach enables you to skip so much of the crap that's involved in indirect game and save time in the process.

You're also subtly putting across to the girl that your time is valuable and that you're a busy guy. Seriously, if you have this mind set then she'll believe it.

Going direct enables you to find out within 5 seconds if she has a boyfriend. You'll know because she'll thank you for the lovely compliment but she has a boyfriend. Caveat: Don't necessarily believe this, it's often simply a natural gut response, we'll discuss this later.

Trust me, by going direct you'll have her instant respect! This is because very few guys have the balls to go direct especially in the middle of the day. You'll have her respect and you'll see it in her face! In fact the only guys who do tend to approach women direct in the middle of the day tend to be homeless men, beggars, charity workers or the occasional drunk who does it to many women no matter what they look like.

While we're here, I may as well point out to you something that I don't recommend you do. I've never actually tried this myself but I've heard from respected PUA's that going direct during the night just doesn't work. In fact it works less than going indirect during the day. This is likely because girls know they look gorgeous on a night out anyway and let's face it, how much balls does it really take to go direct when you're drunk anyway?

No, for meeting women at night, indirect is the better method! But for meeting that special somebody during the day the only method is direct!

Approach Anxiety

I'll only go a little bit into approach anxiety (AA) since I've already written an entire book on that subject! If you suffer from AA then I recommend to you that you give it a look over. The problem with most pick up manuals is that they only ever lightly touch on or even completely skip over AA altogether. The vast majority of guys that are new to pick up suffer from AA in a bad way and I sometimes think it's been so long since the master PUA's had it that they've forgotten all about it.

As I state in the book Destroy Approach Anxiety, it is one of my beliefs that the fear of approaching women anywhere, be it night or day, in the street or in a bar comes from the overloading of information in our heads! Guys who are getting into pick up read all the material they can get their hands on regarding the subject in the hope of finding that one pick up line, that one technique or that one magic bullet that will finally make things easy for them.

It's this reading of so many theories, often contradictory that causes AA. The fact is that to become good at indirect pick up you really do need to know a lot of theory. This will only increase your AA especially if you're new to this. After all, how are you supposed to pull out all these tips, tricks and techniques on your first few approaches whilst you're nervous as hell and under complete pressure? It's impossible! That's why I focus on keeping things as simple as possible.

The reason DDG works so well is mainly because you skip out all the theory and just break the whole approach down to its bare bones. There's no crap flying through your head, there's no trying to remember your next line or routine, it really is just you and her in the moment as real people.

This is another reason why I only advocate for DDG especially for those guys who are just getting started. When you're starting out, you really need the simplest method out there, the method that will get you used to approaching hot women and getting over that fear. If you so desire then later on once you've overcome any AA then you can experiment with indirect approaches and see if it suits you any better. Once you're over your AA then if you so wish, you can start learning NLP, routines, tricks etc as much of that stuff can indeed benefit you, but only if you're already practiced at walking up to women and starting an interaction with them. There is no way in hell any normal guy can pull any of that advanced stuff off on their first few approaches while their knees are shaking and their head is spinning. But I'll also point out too, that none of that "advanced" stuff is really even necessary, especially when using DDG.

Until that time arrives however, then the DDG method is the easiest of all the methods! It is the easiest method because there are very few elements to it. So when you make your approach and you're talking to her in the street with dozens of people walking past you there are very few things that can cause your brain to seize up.

If I remember back to even before I got into pick up, I had more balls approaching girls because I used the direct approach. It was not until I started reading pick up material which advocated for going indirect even out in the street did I suddenly develop a fear of approaching anybody at all. Looking back, it was due to a long list of approach styles, methods, techniques, tips, tricks, games, routines and many more things all bogging my brain down. Whereas if I'd never read anything at all and I just had something like this guide telling me the best way of making direct approaches I could have been years ahead and could have met many more incredible women.

It's true, you've paid money for this book and it's a short book! And I'm doing you a big favour by making it short. I'm doing you an even bigger favour by making it simple and straightforward because when it's all said and done, those are always the approaches that work the best.

Now let's get into the dynamics of the direct daytime approach.

Pre-Approach

Whether you're going out especially to talk to women or if you're just going about your daily business and if anyone catches your fancy you'll be ready to make the approach, it always pays to be prepared. Take these pre-approach measures and when you see your target there's no excuse for not approaching.

Always Look Your Best

One of the things I state in my book Destroy Approach Anxiety is that we always make excuses for not making that approach. A common excuse is that I'm having a bad day, a bad hair day, a bad skin day or I'm simply not wearing my best shoes today.

Don't let any of these silly reasons be the reason why you sissy out of approaching your dream girl on any given day.

If you always step outside the house looking your best then you'll also feel your best. You'll feel more confident and indestructible. At least then you can't make this excuse for copping out on an approach.

No, when we look our best it gives us a great amount of confidence to talk to anybody. We even end up walking differently, more upright when we're dressed in our best clothes. Have you ever noticed that?

Finally, it's no secret the ladies love a well-dressed and well groomed man. So let's not disadvantage ourselves here. By making a direct approach while looking your very best, you're much more likely to end up speaking to a receptive girl.

Be Spontaneous

When you're out and about, I've found it's far easier to approach a girl if you don't make going out to pick up girls your reason for being out in the first place. It's funny, not only do they hardly ever seem to show up when you're searching for them, but you'll also have a constant feeling of nerves coursing through your veins. This will be a likely source of AA not to mention a quivering voice if you actually end up speaking to her.

It's far better to be fully prepared to make the approach whilst you go about your daily business. That way, if you see a nice lady that you want to speak to then you can just snap into approach mode and march straight up to her.

If you worship the 3 second rule then trust me, there is no time for any nervousness or sweat to show itself. In fact you'll be talking to her before you've even really thought about it.

The rule is this: You see her, you're already walking towards her!

Listen To Upbeat Music

This one really is optional, but is also a top tip I have included in Destroy Approach Anxiety as listening to motivational songs can really put you in the mood for making that approach.

Pick songs that are meaningful to you! Do you have any songs that have positive associations for you? Songs that fire you up whenever you hear them? These are the best possible songs to have included on your iPod prior to making that approach. Therefore you can be listening to your song as you're walking up to her and take your ear plugs out just before you open your mouth.

I will include a list of generic motivational songs which I really love below, feel free to disagree, but please remember to include your own:

My Way – Frank Sinatra

Everybody's Free (To Wear Sunscreen) – Baz Luhrmann

Go Your Own Way – Fleetwood Mac / Lissie from the Twinings Ad

I Feel Good – James Brown

Tub Thumping – Chumba Wumba

One Day More – Les Miserables

Nessun Dorma – Pavarotti

Affirmation – Savage Garden

Song 2 – Blur

Beautiful One – Suede

I Won't Back Down – Tom Petty

March On – Good Charlotte (highly recommended)

You Gotta Be – Des'ree

Hero – Mariah Carey

Beautiful Day – U2

Gotta Be Somebody – Nickelback

I Believe I Can Fly – R. Kelly

It's A Beautiful Life – Ace of Base

It's My Life – Bon Jovi

Greatest Day – Take That

Believe – Josh Groban

Eye of the Tiger – Survivor

When you make your direct approach you can even weave one of these songs into it to make the whole thing sound more fun, real and spontaneous. For example: "Hey, I just saw you from over there and I thought to myself, wow, I just have to come over and talk to her or I'd just kick myself!" At this point you introduce yourselves: "I hope you're the friendly type though, because you've just interrupted the chorus of (insert song title here)."

Works a charm!

Confidence – The Most Important Ingredient!

What is the number 1 trait in men that women are attracted to? It's not your money, looks or humour, but your confidence!

What kind of men approach women cold and direct in the street? Confident men is the answer to that! So by the very fact you'll be approaching women in a direct way, they are going to naturally assume you're confident! Therefore, it's very important that you actually are confident about your approach.

Now if you're new to this then unfortunately, and I'm going to be honest with you here, it will take a few approaches and even a few setbacks before you do become confident at approaching.

You need to appear as if you don't give a damn whether or not the approach goes amazingly well or really bad. Confident guys don't care either way because a guy who is confident wouldn't let the outcome of one approach effect his state.

In fact it's incredible how confident you feel after making one approach during any given day. You'll be floating around for the rest of the day I guarantee you, especially in the early stages. This is true even if your approach goes very badly! You should utilize this high to make even more approaches off the back of the first one.

For those who think looking and sounding confident will be an issue, you'll be pleased to know that faking confidence is actually quite easy. Just follow these tips:

- First and foremost, as already mentioned, confident men dress well, they are well groomed and this in turn gives them even more confidence. When you are dressed really well have you ever noticed how you stand and walk differently, with your head held high? This leads to our next point.

- You need to ensure you walk upright with excellent posture. This in itself will give you power which you'll feel running through your body. You need to walk with your chin up, shoulders pulled back, chest out a little bit, pull your tummy in and walk with a deliberate purpose. If you struggle with this then just imagine there is a helium balloon attached to your chin and its pulling your entire head upwards. That always seems to do the trick.

- Make no apologies for approaching your targets and interrupting their day. You're a man, you've seen somebody attractive that you'd like to talk to and it's them that should be thankful for it.

- When you finally speak to her, it's vitally important you speak in a slow and controlled manner. Confident people speak slowly because they don't expect anybody will interrupt them. Try it when you next speak to your friends. Experiment speaking fast and speaking slowly. See which makes you sound more in control of the situation. Speaking slowly will make you

21

sound much more authoritative. It will also serve to allay your nerves (for reasons I'll talk about more in the approach section), which will in turn prevent the girl from becoming nervous in your presence.

- When you speak, alternate the pitch of your voice. Very few people speak with varying pitches and it's a very interesting and even attractive trait. Listen to how news readers, game show hosts or even movie stars speak and try and learn from them. This will make you appear captivating, not to mention confident.

- It is very important when you speak to use body language. Body language shows you're in control of the situation and are not afraid to take up a little bit of space. Simply bend your arms at the elbows and make small gestures while talking. You can make slightly larger gestures when you emphasize a point. Practice doing this in the mirror. Be careful not to overdo it though or it could look a little staged.

- When you're standing there, widen your stance and take up a little extra space. This shows your dominance and makes you appear more rooted.

- Your movements need to be slow and controlled. Again, only confident people make slow movements, like nothing in the world bothers them. Just think how fast and erratic movements make people seem nervous. Make sure you do the opposite.

- A simple thing for you not to do is to cross or fold your arms. This makes you appear defensive and uncomfortable. Remember to keep your arms bent at the elbow, perhaps even clasp your hands together in front of you.

- An obvious tip is not to fidget. Many people fidget without even realising it and it always blows your cover as a confident man. Keep your hands away from your face and resist the urge to play with your phone; not that you would in a pick up situation.
- Confident men make eye contact! This is obvious!

The crazy thing is, and studies have proven this, that if you project these confident mannerisms, not only do you look confident in the eyes of other people, but you actually feel the confidence within yourself. It's a case of life imitating art!

An easy way of explaining this in a more practical sense is that when you have your arms crossed you actually feel more closed off. However when you unfold your arms, you naturally open up.

In fact one technique I can give you now for when you're next speaking to a girl; If she has her arms crossed then you'll notice that you really can get her to open up more and become more talkative to you if you can somehow get her to unfold her arms. You can do this by introducing yourself and shaking her hand or even by giving her a high five if she says something you agree with or find really interesting. Seldom will she ever refold her arms because she should no longer feel so defensive.

If you've done everything listed above for your pre-approach, then if she happens to see you walking up to her, her opinion should be fairly warm and receptive once you actually start speaking. Remember that women rarely get approached by good groomed and well intentioned guys throughout the day. What they do get is plenty of homeless looking men, drunks and vagabonds. Use this fact to your advantage.

The Approach

Now we're getting into the nitty gritty, the actual approach and reason you bought this book. Remember that this whole book is about direct game during the day time. The whole structure is surprisingly simple, which is of course the best way. The DDG approach will work just about anywhere during the day, the main places being; the street, the coffee shop, shopping mall and college or university campus. All you have to do is tailor the DDG approach to your current venue as necessary but trust me, there's really not much difference.

I will state a little something here. I know from running my website www.howtopickupwomen.org that I have had many, many search engine queries for terms such as "pick up women at the gym" or "gym pick up." It has become my belief through having tried direct game at the gym a few times that DDG isn't the best approach for that kind of environment. In my opinion it's because women know they look great at the gym and it kind of comes over as creepy by having a direct approach in that situation. I think that gym pick up is a topic for another day and perhaps even a book in itself. But I've been given the opinion by people I trust and respect that the best method is more indirect and perhaps even indirect over a longer period of time. This is because the gym environment is closer to that of a bar at night than in the street during the day and so it requires its own category. A worthy digression perhaps!

Now let's take a good look at the actual DDG approach. If you're sceptical about the thought of marching straight up to a woman you've never seen or spoken to before and telling her you think she's stunning then I at least urge you to keep an open mind. Most importantly please make sure you give it a few tries. The thought of being one of the few guys who can actually do this is actually completely empowering!

Walking Towards Her

The majority of the time, you'll see your target walking along the street. Remember the three second rule; you see her, you're already walking towards her!

If the street is quiet then you can just go straight over to her no hesitations. In fact by following her on a quiet street, you're seriously going to risk being arrested. If it's busy then you can follow her for a few paces and try and time it so you can get into an opening, but this is really optional. Some guys would prefer to have fewer people around when they stop the girl but trust me, you shouldn't let other people hold the key to your own private prison cell.

Please guys, never approach her from behind, it hardly ever achieves good results. No tapping her on the shoulder from her blind spot either. You have to get in front of her! If she's walking away from you then this will probably involve walking around her in an arc so you appear in front. This is very important: Make sure you give her plenty of room!

When you stop in front of her and I do mean in front, not from the side and not from behind then you need to give her around two whole metres of space. To put it in perspective, it should be the length of you lying down on the floor and then another half of you added to that. The reason for this is twofold. Firstly, it'll make her feel more comfortable. Homeless guys, beggars and charity muggers give girls no room when they make their approaches. Partly why they seldom have any luck! You need to come across as different.

Secondly, the girl will not be expecting to be approached. She will almost certainly carry on walking for a few paces before her brain even realises there's anybody in front of her. Actually I wouldn't stop bang on in front of her, but with a tiny angle of say 20 degrees so it feels less intimidating for her.

Sometimes, you may even have to run to get in front of her, especially if she's walking with a purpose. Don't worry, the direct approach is all about impact and this will add to the impact and make everything appear more spontaneous. Though if she is walking fast then you'll need to give her even more than two metres to avoid her clattering into you.

If you've seen many live in field day game videos on Youtube (and I recommend you watch some) then you'll probably have no idea that actually getting the girl to stop is the hardest part of the pick up. In fact these videos rarely show you footage of the girls who don't stop to talk to them.

Remember, it's very important to have complete belief in yourself! If she detects a hint of nervousness or doubt then you'll come across as weak and quite possibly as just another beggar who's asking for money. Know in your head that she's going to stop for you and 9 times out of ten they always do! On the off chance that she doesn't stop for you, don't feel bad, you've not been rejected, she just rejected your actual approach and not you as a person. Simply analyse the actual walk up to her and see where you could have improved. The most likely answer is that you simply didn't give her enough room in front. Another important thing is to never ever go along with the rest of the pick up for a girl who refused to stop for you. Remember that to go out on a limb and tell a girl how stunning you think she is is to give her a wonderful, magical gift. If she doesn't deserve it then don't give her it! It's a special gift and you're giving it to special people! So make sure you only give it to girls who stop and not to the back of a girl who carried on walking.

For the shopping mall, this is a whole lot easier. Often she'll be stood still window shopping or at the most, walking rather slow weighed down by all her shopping bags. Just remember to give her the same amount of space.

For the coffee shop you can of course walk closer to her because she'll be sat down. You can even stoop down to her level or gesture to a nearby chair to say "I'm sitting here!"

On the very rare occasion you may even see a nice girl on crutches! Take full advantage of this because she's not getting away from you! Seriously guys, don't waste these gifts that occur only a few times in an average year even in a big city.

The key thing to remember in all cases is to be dominant and unapologetic about interrupting her day!

Stopping Her

Right, you've walked in front of her, you now need to get her to stop.

This part is simple! All you need to do is gesture for her to stop with your hands. Your hands need to be tilted to a non-threatening 45 degree angle, make your fingers go limp and spread them out a little. Your hands should be level with her stomach. This is extremely none-threatening yet you're still blocking her path with your hands. By the way, your hands should offset the 20 degree angle you gave her in that your body is slightly out of her way, but your arms are blocking her course, albeit in the none-threatening way I've just explained.

Following on from the step above, when you angle round on her and make your turn, you'll naturally have one foot in front of the other. This looks cooler, more natural and less threatening because I also suggest you lean backwards over your rear foot. You should practice this a little with an imaginary moving target. Try and pull off the whole manoeuvre in a smooth way and so of course, you really should practice it in private.

Now you've made your move, it's time to open your mouth and say your first words. You should do this as you tilt backwards over your rear foot in one smooth motion with an "excuse me," "hey," "hi" etc.

This is the point where she should stop for you! Remember that if she doesn't stop then just let her go and don't say anything more. Don't give her your magical gift! But you have to have 100% belief that she's going to stop and nine times of out ten they always do!

Your Direct Opener

So you've just said your pre-opener (hey, hi, excuse me) and she has stopped for you. Try and relate to what is going through her mind at this moment. She has no idea what is about to happen and if you rush into your opening line then chances are it's all going to be in a blur for her. So after you've said hi, wait a couple of seconds for her to find her feet.

Now the beauty of the direct opener is that you can use the same modified line over and over again in almost any situation. You should tailor it to suit you and try and make it sound spontaneous and dramatic like the following:

"Hey, I was just walking along over there and I saw you and I thought, oh my god she is stunning, I just had to come over and say hi and see if you were friendly as well."

Or...

"Hey, I was just stood over there with my friends and I saw you and I thought wow she is stunning, I literally just had to run away from them to say hi to you. I hope you're friendly too?"

Or for the coffee shop...

"Hey, I just saw you as I was queuing up for my latte and I thought to myself, oh my god, she looks absolutely stunning and so I just had to come over and say hi and find out if you were friendly too? May I take a seat?"

You can see that all direct openers involve putting your heart on your sleeve and declaring your intention straight away!

You're a man remember, this is what real men do and don't apologise for it!

If you're sharp eyed you will have noticed that all of these openers involve asking if she is friendly too. I'm using a little bit of psychology here that I will explain in a bit.

I will also reiterate here that your opener needs to be delivered slowly and calmly. It's so easy to do this too quickly and risk coming over as nervous in the process. Please practice getting your voice speed and tone right with a few dummy runs somewhere private. Another thing that I used to find happen to me was that my voice would go a little too high which would also betray my nerves. Try and deepen your voice a little. I'm being totally serious when I say that the way you make your direct opener should really sound even more slow than what would sound normal or natural. You will have your line in your head and if you say it slowly and calmly, you're less likely to stutter over it. You'll also sound ten times more relaxed and confident, which will make her feel relaxed, which will (trust me) further make you relaxed. You'll be in a conversation with this girl and you will feed off each other. Moods can be contagious and this all stems from the very first words that come from your mouth. I completely understand that many of you reading this will be nervous as hell, especially when making your first approaches, but you really can improve your entire bearing simply by doing such a simple thing that you really should practice; Slow and Calm!

Remember to make eye contact.

The Introduction

So after you've stated your opening line, now is the right time to introduce yourselves. Tell her what your name is and hold out your hand. Now remember that you're probably still up to two whole metres away from her so of course use this opportunity to get a little closer. Shake her hand and tell her what your name is, she should respond with hers. I like to hold on to the hand for longer than a usual hand shake, but obviously not too long that it becomes creepy. Use your best judgement.

After you've shaken hands you really don't need to put much thought into how close to stand to her, the aim is to get into a normal conversation so just do what is comfortable for you both.

Possible Objection

Because you've used a direct opener, it is obvious what your intention is. So it is at this point that the girl will usually thank you for your interest but say she has a boyfriend, assuming of course that she actually has a boyfriend. After all, wouldn't you want your girlfriend to say to somebody reading this book that she had a boyfriend if that was the case?

However, this is often an instinctual reaction given to ward of the lower value men. Remember the shit test from earlier? Well it still exists during the day, albeit in a much weaker fashion.

You should never let this affect your game plan. My typical answer to the boyfriend response is simply to say in a nice, playful tone "you don't have a boyfriend."

At this point she will either say "I have" in an equally playful tone, or she will tend to smile and ask you your name or some other question. Either way, you'll know the truth of the situation pretty soon.

I have been known in the past to carry on speaking to the girl regardless of the boyfriend. I'm after all just out being friendly and you're still going to be on a massive high after speaking to her for a few minutes. You never know, you may have a hobby or job in common and you could make a new acquaintance in the process. But if she does indeed have a boyfriend then you must be respectful, I'm sure you will be!

Post Opener – Transition

After actually getting your target to stop, it is the transition which is the hardest part of the direct pick up. This is because you've finished with the only scripted part of the pick up and you're on your own. Your brain has also just realised you're speaking to a hot girl in the street and the nerves are only now starting to kick in. It's not uncommon for you to physically feel your knees shaking from this point until the end of the pick up. I've had this happen many times, but trust me, it gets a lot easier. Another thing that used to happen was that my foot would involuntarily tap on the floor. The best course of action to take is simply to ignore it.

The transition really involves you bridging the gap between your opener and a normal conversation. Her head may still be coming to terms with what is happening so the transition is used to give her a few extra seconds for her brain to adjust to the fact she's being approached by a nice guy, friendly guy.

The transition should involve you making some kind of a comment or statement that is specific to her. It should ideally not be a question, which is too easy to do, but should instead be a comment or statement.

What was it specifically about her that you liked? What was it about her that caught your eye?

Now would be a great time to say what it was. "I really like your scarf" or "You just walk like you're on a mission" or "You don't see many girls around here with such a unique sense of style!" That last one is always a good one to use!

You could even say something funny to lighten the situation and put both of you at ease, in fact if you're able to do this then that really would be the best approach. "You should slow down while you walk, I had to sprint to catch up with you" or "You made me ditch my friends, you'd better be worth it" or "Wow, you're making me do this in the middle of Starbucks, I can't believe you!"

This makes the whole approach seem all the more real and spontaneous which means that by the end of it you should have a pretty receptive and open girl.

The Conversation

You know what? Once you've gotten over the very slight stumbling block that is the transition phase, the next goal is simply to get into an everyday normal conversation with the girl.

You don't really need to know a great deal of tips and tricks as the whole point of DDG is to keep the whole structure as simple as possible. Of course I'll include a few strategies to help you out but the emphasis at least in the early stages should be to approach as many nice girls as possible and get over any AA if you happen to have AA. Once you are past any AA you might have then you can and should incorporate some more advanced methods into your arsenal to give yourself a few extra tools. Remember that it is my belief that it is the overloading of these tools that causes AA in the first place, so please ensure you get over your fear of approaching (assuming that's the case) before you fill your head with other pick up material.

There are no rules to how short or long the conversation should be but as a general rule, the longer the conversation the more solid a phone number will be when she gives you it. Don't expect a girl to be as receptive to a phone call or text message from you following a two minute conversation as she would be following a twenty minute convo.

You should use this time to get to know her, what she likes and try to find some common ground. Finding common ground is very important for the purpose of actually arranging a date. Of course you can arrange to meet at a bar or for coffee but if you both really love art galleries for example then that would be the logical place to have a first date. So keep this in mind.

I know how easy it is for our minds to go blank when we're in these situations, but most of the time the girl will be happy to take up some of the slack for you. I find that in the vast majority of cases, I actually struggle to get a word in myself. However, just in case here are some things you can ask to keep the conversation moving along while trying to find out a little more about her at the same time:

- Ask her what she was doing before you interrupted her.
- What area of town is she from?
- What does she study/do for work?
- What does she like doing if she has a full day for herself?

It really is that simple! The final question in the list above is excellent for finding out what she actually likes to do.

If you don't actually have anything in common and you still really like her then of course a bar or coffee shop is the best option to take.

In the past, if I've had absolutely nothing in common with the girl, I've been known to thank her for her time and to move on.

You might think I'm insane for doing that, but there is an important lesson and psychological shift right there. I am putting myself in the position of selector! We guys know all too well that it's mainly down to the women, who have men throwing themselves at them all the time to pick and choose which guy she wants to date. The rare guy who comes along, who does the picking and choosing himself is actually a rare find.

You should go into your approaches with the mind-set that that girl on the other side of the street is hot, I wonder if we have anything in common. This puts you in a powerful position and actually gives you most of the power in the interaction.

Getting the Phone Number

Remember that it's actually quite important to have found common ground before you go for the phone number. You have to make it as logical as possible to meet up again because you both share a common interest. Of course if none can be found, you always have bars and coffee shops to fall back on and there's no real harm in that.

Assuming you've both just discovered you like art galleries, art house movies or Italian food you can then just say to her that you should both go to the art gallery/movie theatre or new Italian restaurant in town. There's no need to ask her, just tell her! "We should both go to the art gallery!" Then hand the girl your phone and tell her "Put your digits in there!"

Doing this will make you seem like a very confident guy and completely in control of the situation, a trait all women admire in men, it is confidence after all. There really is no reason to ask a girl for her phone number, you really do need to take a lead and tell her, not ask!

While she's inputting her digits, a common mistake many guys make is to keep silent while she's doing it. I'm sure you've noticed in the past that a girl putting her number in your phone is quite a heavy moment, for you both actually. You should try and lighten the moment a little by continuing your conversation while she's inputting her digits. If she has a friend with her then talk to the friend!

Another common mistake and I've made this one myself more than once is to end the interaction and to rush off as soon as you have the number. Getting the number is not the prize here, but actually getting the girl on a date. You still have work to do after getting the number.

If you've found common ground then getting the number should be a logical extension of that common ground, but you were still talking before about a range of issues so why not carry on talking about whatever it was to strengthen the chances of her texting you back, or answering your call.

However, if you really want to improve your odds of being able to see her in a more social setting then the next section will really increase your chances!

Instant Dates

Instant dates (ID's) refer to meeting a girl and then going for coffee there and then. They are surprisingly easy to carry out.

You have after all shown your worth and approached her cold and direct in the middle of a busy street in the middle of the day. You've made your introductions and chatted for a few minutes. You know she's a friendly type of girl and she knows you're a great guy, in fact a very rare guy with balls.

Going for a coffee there and then is only logical and as long as she is not busy she should jump at the offer. For this reason, it's actually quite important you find out if you interrupted an important engagement or her going to work for example. If you could tell she was shopping then there's no way she'll have a problem with going for a coffee with you as she'll have time on her hands.

Getting a phone number during an ID will provide you with the strongest possible chance of being able to see her again. As long as she likes you, girls who give you their phone number during in ID rarely ever flake. This is because they have already invested quite a bit of time into you and you're far from just another guy she met in the street. You're probably the only guy in her life that she met and went for a spontaneous coffee with. It's all very romantic and women love that kind of thing. Trust me, when she gets home she'll be telling all her friends about this!

Being on an ID with a girl is no different to being on an actual date with her! I have written a full book on dating psychology for men; First Date Tips for Men, which is filled with subtle psychological strategies you can use to make her fall hook, line and sinker for you whilst you're having your date.

Don't be surprised if the girl offers to pay for you! This happens frequently and you should let her. By allowing the girl to invest her time, effort and now money into you, you are making yourself subtly a more enticing catch. We do after all value what we have to work for, or invest in.

One of the most powerful things you can do during your ID is to "qualify" the girl! I'm going to lift the section on qualification from my book First Date Tips for Men into the next section for you to study. This is powerful stuff and will really make the difference for you. If you manage to get a girl on an ID, something which you should really go for then I urge you to use qualification!

Bonus Strategies

- Qualification
- I Hope You're Friendly Too?
- Pre Approach Priming

QUALIFICATION

Now I'm tempted to say that qualification is even more important than forging a connection with the girl, but for the simple reason that you won't get to qualification or really even need it if you build a good connection, I'm still putting the earlier section at the top of my list.

Once again, I will reiterate that building a connection is the most important thing to make a girl want to see you again.

But let's change the mind-set for this section. For qualification is where YOU decide if you want to see HER again.

Qualification is something women are very, very good at!

They do it naturally! They do it all the time simply because they grow up with an expectation of what their dream guy should be like! Even if later on in their lives they become realistic as to what men actually are, when they are younger, girls still have this high expectation of what they want in a boyfriend or of men in general.

In fact it's tough luck for any guy who doesn't meet this high expectation.

In fact it's become a lot harder for us guys to "qualify" to their high expectations all thanks to Sex and the City and countless romantic comedies starring Jennifer Aniston, but I won't bore you by ranting on about that!

To put it simply, girls have in their heads a list of what we have to be like in order for them to be interested in us. It usually looks something like this:

1. Sense of humour
2. He MUST be a Doctor, Lawyer or run his own successful business
3. He must get me
4. He must be caring and sensitive
5. He must have an incredible body
6. He must be handsome
7. All my friends must also love him

This list will probably run on and on. The thing is that the hotter the girl, in most cases the longer the list.

In fact, girls will often go out of their way to find this information out about us and they'll be completely unapologetic about it too!

Take a typical conversation on the average first date:

Girl: So what is it you do?

Guy: I'm doing an apprenticeship with Auto Mechanics in town! / I work for the tax department / I'm an administrator!

Girl: Oh so how long have you been doing that?

Guy: About 2 years!

Girl: But you're also at Uni as well right? You are aiming for higher things yes?

Guy: Ermm well errmmm no.

In fact the guy above sensing the girls disappointment with what he does, seeing he could now lose her has to try hard to make up lost ground! But it's already too late!

Once he has to try to get her to like him again, it's already game over in most situations!

She has qualified him to her expectations and he did not match up to what she wants in a man!

The only way I can see him turning this around would be to show how proud he is of doing what he's doing. Showing how he's making a difference etc. Then bide his time and qualify her to HIS standards!

This is often hard for us guys! Remember her list above? Well this is a typical guys list:

1. She must be hot!

Is it any wonder why girls have a big advantage over us? Is it any wonder why it so often appears like it's them that get to do all the picking and choosing instead of us guys!

Qualification is something that all women do! The hotter the woman the worse it gets!

But what if we could play them at their own game? What if we could qualify them to our ridiculously high standards of what we need in a woman for us to even consider them!

Well fortunately this is very easy once you understand the principles! We can play them at their own game and frustrate the hell out of them in the process!

You will find that if you're dating a not so hot girl, you won't need to apply much qualification. But trust me, as they get hotter, the more you'll need to qualify them!

If you're dating a girl who dates lots of guys, this is going to make you stand out so far and above any other guy she's ever met!

The first thing we need to do is make a list, just like how they have! You don't have to actually write it down, but just know what it is you want in a girl.

I mean it! What do you actually want in a girl?

This only really works if it's something not related in the slightest to her looks! Make sure that you're the only guy she's ever met who couldn't give a damn about her looks! The looks are just a bonus! What you really want, what you really need in a girl is what you have on your list!!!

1. She must be ambitious!
2. She mustn't smoke!
3. She must not be the one who simply follows all her mates, but does her own thing.
4. She can hold a conversation.

5. She's clever.
6. She likes to travel and discover new places.
7. She can't be materialistic, I need a girl who can be happy without all those flashy things.
8. She has to be spontaneous! I need someone who can run out in the rain with me when it thunders and just go crazy!

You see what a list like this does?

It doesn't matter how attractive she is! If she doesn't tick your boxes on this list then she doesn't get a look in! You'll be the only guy she's ever known who would turn her down simply because she's not spontaneous!

Hot girls are used to having all the power!

Now you've just taken that power away from her!

And because of this, she has no choice but to chase YOU!!!

And she WILL chase you!!!

She'll chase you because you're different, you're the only guy she's ever met that isn't drooling over her!

You're the only guy she's ever met who's used qualification!!!

So...now you have your list! How best to use this list?

Well the best way to use this magical list is to be blunt and just ask her!

Remember that the contents of this list are very important to you. So why not just ask her? She asked you about your job right? So play her at her own game!

Guy: You know, you're quite funny which I really like and you can hold a conversation too! But what I really want to know is if you're the kind of girl who just loves discovering new places?

You need to make it look like it's important to you!

Disclaimer: You need to have built up a certain amount of rapport and have made at least some connection before using this! Otherwise she's not going to care whether she conforms to your standards or not!

No girl in the world is going to say "no" she doesn't like discovering new places! The fact is it doesn't matter! You're qualifying her based on something other than her looks and so far she's passing your tests!

After this initial little bit of qualification I would wait a while before trying it again. You could in the meantime find out what places she's discovered recently! And I'm not talking about the new nail painting place down the road!

By getting her to "explain herself" to you, by trying to impress you by telling you of the places she's discovered, you're forcing her to make a big effort to impress you.

Wait a few minutes and then throw in the big one, the money shot, the deal breaker!

Girl: So that's where I always go to get my nails done these days!

Guy: That's fine! Are you spontaneous??? I really like spontaneous people!!!

Again, no girl in the world is going to say she's not spontaneous. Even most guys like to think of themselves as being spontaneous, it is after all another word for exciting is it not?

Let's go back to the conversation where we left off!

Girl: Oh well erm, yes I suppose I am spontaneous!!!

Guy: Awesome! Tell me one really spontaneous thing you've done in the last six months?

Now just sit back and wait for her reply!

Remember to make it look like it's important to you that she's spontaneous. It has to seem to her like it's possible that the answer she gives might disappoint you. And that is an extremely important part of it!

If she gives a typical girly answer which is not something that excites you then you need to act genuinely disappointed (breaking rapport)!

Girl: Well I was bored last week so I just phoned my friend up and we drove 50 miles to the next town for a shopping trip!

Guy: That's rubbish! Give me something else! Something really cool that's going to impress me!

Girl: OK well a few weeks ago I was walking by a sign that said "join up for fencing lessons" and I thought, that's so cool, I've just got to give it a go, so I did!

The important thing is that if it sounds genuinely impressive, then you need to be impressed and you need to let her know how cool it is that she did what she did and that she has your approval!

Equally important is that if it's a load of crap and you're not impressed one bit then you have to tell her that that's nothing (in a half jokey, yet half serious way) and she's going to have to try harder to come up with something a little better!

Seriously! What you're doing is getting HER to impress YOU!

Think about all the times there's been girls you've liked in the past. You've gone out of your way to impress them by boasting about your exploits and everything else. What this tends to do in most cases is turn the girl off!

By the very fact that you're trying so hard to impress the girl, shows that she has you in her control, she has very little she needs to do to get you.

By phrasing your questions correctly and by being a little manipulative, you're actually turning the tables and getting her to impress you. Don't be turned off though like she would. You've been very clever and so you should reap the rewards.

When we try hard to impress somebody, it's because we really like them! We try to impress people because we want them to like us too. Qualification is how you get them to try and impress YOU, because on a deep down level you've positioned yourself slightly above them and they need to demonstrate that they are on your level.

By using qualification on a girl you're pretty much, for lack of a better expression, forcing her to impress you. If she's trying to impress you, then she must clearly like you!

This is how the rich ugly guy gets the gorgeous girl. Because rich guys naturally use qualification all the time. They've already been there and done that, they've got the car to prove it. If a girl is even to get a look in, then they're going to have to prove they're worth the effort.

One thing about girls, especially really hot girls is that they're very competitive! They have huge egos and this is how you use it to your advantage!

I Hope You're Friendly Too?

Have you ever asked a girl if she's friendly?

If so then what did she say?

Did she say that no she wasn't friendly? I doubt it!

By working the question or statement "I hope you're friendly?" into your opening line you are in fact commanding to her that she be friendly to you!

"Hey, I was just over there with my friends and I saw you and I thought to myself, oh my god she is just stunning, and I just had to come over and say hi and see if you were friendly too!?"

You've already shown your worth by making this ballsy approach and now you're asking/demanding of her that she shows her worth and be friendly to you!

No girl in the world is going to be a bitch after you've paid her such a fine compliment, it's just not polite. You're also subtly putting across to her that you like friendly people! In fact you should phrase this statement more as a question that you tag on to the end of your direct opening line.

In fact you can use this incredible technique again later on in your interaction by telling her "hey, you know what I really like about you...I've only just met you but you're just so friendly!"

I will explain the dynamic behind this by lifting a section from my book First Date Tips for Men, a dating psychology guide for men.

Start vvv

Ok so now we're getting into some super psychological areas of the human mind which we can exploit to our benefit! What you're about to find out is the most effective way of complimenting a girl.

What you're about to learn here works incredibly well on first dates! But more than that it works like a charm in pick up situations too, if you're into pick up at all, which you should be. If you're in a bar, night club or even approaching a girl on the street then this technique can change things around in your favour with incredibly awesome power.

To explain this properly I'm going to have to try and relate it to something you will hopefully have experienced in your own life!

When I was a kid, I wasn't anything special; I was always a follower and was easily manipulated by anyone! Below is one of the ways it was done, although I doubt in all honesty they knew what they were doing at the time!

We used to play Soccer in the park nearly every day. Nobody ever wanted to be the goal keeper as it's boring! But the sneaky bastards could always have me volunteering to be the keeper and they did it like this...

Friend: You're really good in nets aren't you! You're fearless…I've never seen anyone so willing to stand in front of a Football coming for your face at such high speed.

Me: Thanks!

Friend: Yeah you can dive really far as well; it's dead hard to score against you!

Now what my friends did was to complement me in an honest and sincere way! What's more is that they went into a little bit of detail as to WHY I was so good as a goalkeeper. For me this meant that I didn't want to disappoint them by altering this image they had of my goalkeeping skills.

Heck, I would even go as far as practicing my dives in my spare time so I could dive even further so I wouldn't alter that image they had of me as a fearless goalkeeper who could dive far!

Did your older Brother ever once say to you "I love you, you're so generous with your pocket money!"

This is the exact technique that older Brothers have been using to fleece younger Brothers of their pocket money for centuries!

So how can you use this to your advantage in the dating arena?

Well timing is important! It has to sound sincere and genuine for it to work, so pulling this out the bag when you've only been talking 2 minutes isn't going to work! You can however bring it out of the bag after about 5 minutes ☺. You'll have to use your best judgement!

Girl: So I went shopping with Sarah and we bought these new gloves, I've never seen gloves like them I just had to have them.

Guy: You know what...I can see why Sarah likes you so much...you're just so friendly! I've only known you a few minutes but you immediately make people feel at ease! That's a very rare thing in people these days!

Now girls don't ever get compliments from guys like this, they usually compliment them on their looks so you'll stand out again by doing this!

But you've just given her a sincere compliment about how friendly she is! Now unless you give her a good reason not to be friendly to you she's going to try her very best to keep this image of what you have of her in your mind! She's not going to want to disappoint you by being unfriendly!

Now can you see how this could also work in a pick up situation?

Girls are often very uneasy with pick ups and for good reason; they're just not practiced at being picked up during the day! By using this technique while picking girls up you're practically commanding her to be friendly to you! It never fails to amaze me watching a girl who's nervous and closed up suddenly become friendly, talkative and chatty simply because you've told her sincerely how friendly she is!

You need to have been talking to her for long enough so that you've come up with a reason why she's friendly! The reason is very important because if you don't have a reason why she's friendly then there's no way it can be genuine. She'll see through it in an instant!

End ^^^

I wrote that with the first date or an ID in mind, but it really can be used just as well during a pick up situation. Give it a try and see how well it works!

Pre Approach Priming

Pre approach priming (PAP) is not something that you'll be able to carry out all that often during the day time. It is something that is perhaps a little more suited to night game. That is not to say that you cannot use it during the day, it's just a little harder.

DDG involves approaching women cold, meaning that you've had no prior contact with them. By using PAP you are warming your approach up a tiny bit in order to increase the chances of having a successful approach.

PAP can be something that is as small as eye contact, to a smile, eye contact and a smile or even a hello or a wave. This is something that many women will even instigate.

So why would women instigate what I call PAP? Because they want you to approach them! It's just not the done thing for women to approach guys, that's not how things work unfortunately for us. But that's not to say that women can't give guys subtle signals which are intended to invite us to approach them. This is in fact something that women do on a regular basis. In fact when you're out and about, you should become aware of any PAP signals women are sending you.

When you're walking around, try and make eye contact with as many attractive women as you can. Keep an eye out for those who match your eye contact and smile! That is your invitation to go and approach! You should not hesitate, just do it!

In fact because you've been "invited" to make the approach, you can even skip the direct opener itself and just go straight up to her and introduce yourself. I've done this many, many times in the street, in the shopping mall and in the best place of all for this; the coffee shop.

You can even take things a step further while in the coffee shop. You can make eye contact with her right from the other side of the room, smile and even wave to her. Trust me, if she waves back, which she most often will do then that is your invite to just casually walk up to her and take the seat opposite. Have you ever known approaching women to be this easy?

I read a study somewhere, I wish I could remember where it was, but it was discovered that toddlers who can't yet speak bond much quicker to people they've been waving to across the play pen. If you can get into a "conversation" across the room using any kind of none verbal communication, you're already going to feel very attached to the girl when you sit down next to her, and the feeling will be mutual. Just take the seat and introduce yourself, there's no need for any openers!

You can see how this would work in a bar too, through the loud music, sometimes none verbal communication is the only way to communicate.

You can see why this perhaps doesn't carry over to the street very well because you're both in motion but if you can just get some level of eye contact and a smile from her (you must smile first, or say hi as you pass) then this should be all you need. Your approach is no longer cold and you've set yourself up for an extremely warm reception when you turn round, run up to her and say hi!

PAP is something you can also use in the gym if you happen to make eye contact with a girl. You can simply motion something with your arms, perhaps you could pretend to bench press thin air, or just simply wave to her. Bang, you've just warmed up an approach.

One time I was across the street from an attractive girl and the little green man was taking ages to light up. We made eye contact, then I tapped a pretend watch on my wrist and made the universal yawning and I'm sleeping hand signals. She laughed! So instead of actually crossing the road, I waited at my side for her to approach me and I simply said, "Hi, I'm Charlie!"

The best thing is that it takes zero balls to do this! And the other thing is that if any PAP signals you send out to the girl are not reciprocated then you really haven't lost anything, you haven't even made an approach.

Be creative with your PAP's! Tailor them to your situation and have fun with them. If the girl can see you're smiling and having fun with it, making signals to her from across the crowded coffee shop then she really is going to be open to you when you take the seat opposite her. You're already in a coffee shop too (assuming that's where you are) so I guess you can call this an ID too.

Wow look how far we've come along!

Troubleshooting

Question: I've had a few attempts trying to get girls to stop but their eyes always just glaze over and they just carry on walking! What am I doing wrong?

The most likely reason is that you're not projecting yourself enough. Remember that you've seen something you really want! You have to show this in your approach! Be passionate and dramatic. Project yourself! Be confident! Have belief that she'll stop for you! This is a common thing when starting out but it really is the hardest part of the pick up getting them to stop in the first place. Have a think about what it is you're doing wrong, analyse every approach and think about how you could have done it better.

If it's none of the above it's possible you're not giving the girl enough room in front. Remember you need to give her a minimum of two whole metres, but you should give her even more room if she's walking fast.

If you're still struggling with this then get a friend to give feedback on your approach. Failing that, there are always shopping malls and coffee shops where the targets tend to move slower or are sat down.

Question: Ok, I've given this a few goes and I've had some good success when girls are on their own, but what do I do if the girl I like is with a friend?

It should not affect you at all! That's the advantage of day game over night game, there are different rules. The friend will be polite and hopefully happy her friend is being chatted up. I do though often give a compliment to the other girl as well so she doesn't feel left out and you should try and talk to them both. My initial approach might be tailored differently if there is a friend. I would perhaps pick out something unique about the girl I liked and mention that I liked those qualities. I would approach and say something like "Hey I just saw you over there and I just had to come over and say hi, because I think you're stunning!" I would then say to her friend "I think you're really attractive too, I've just always had a thing for girls with (mention the hair colour of the girl you like)." This way you've given both girls a compliment but also a justified reason why you're choosing her friend. There's no way the friend could be bitter or jealous after that, but do remember to involve her in the conversation as well so she doesn't feel left out.

Question: What if there are two friends?

No difference! And congratulations if you have the guts to do this!

Question: What if we're in a really crowded and busy room or there are just too many people around and I'm worried about embarrassing her?

Well this sounds to me like this is all in your head! Stop being so paranoid, nobody gives a damn about what you're doing! Nobody would believe it anyway!

I don't care if you're in a crowded subway carriage, why are you letting these people dictate what you're going to do? Answer me this, the next day when you're still regretting not approaching that girl because of all the people standing around you, are you still going to even remember these other people in the room? Are you still going to care about them while you're thinking about the girl you let go?

Question: What if the girl I really like is talking on her cell/mobile phone? This happens way too often!

You're right and it's a constant irritation of mine! When I started out, I actually took a DDG private class, just me and an instructor, in fact I took a few of these classes. It cost a lot of money! The advice I was given was to approach her regardless of the mobile phone. You're a man right who's busy and her speaking to her Mum/friend/boss shouldn't make a difference. But after giving it a few tries myself and watching the instructor try as well, I've come to the conclusion that it hardly ever works. For the simple reason that it's rude! Would you like being approached while you're on the phone? Put yourself in the girl's position for a minute!

No, I wouldn't approach her while she's on her phone! Why make things harder than they need to be? The reason DDG works so well is because it's simple, so I keep it simple!

I have been known to follow her, even up to five minutes waiting for her to hang up before making my move, there's not a whole lot else you can do I'm afraid. I've also been known to get fed up waiting for some girls to hang up and I've given up the pursuit. Do you really want a girl who spends her life on the phone anyway?

I'm sure the world's best pick up artists would have no problem with this, but I'm trying to teach the average guy here, normal people! It's up to you; you can give it a few goes if you like. If you really like her then why not, but my opinion is that why should you make DDG any more difficult for yourself when there are stunning girls sat down reading books in Starbucks. Start easy and build up from there!

Question: The only time I get out of the office to do some DDG is at lunchtime when all the girls are eating. I hate the thought of approaching girls while they're eating!

Yes me too! I think it bothers us guys more than it bothers the women though! Similar to the cell phone, wait for her to finish! Always use your common sense in these situations!

Question: I stopped this girl in the street and she has a boyfriend, but I really like her! Any extra tips you can give?

Well put yourself in the position of the boyfriend. How would you feel if somebody reading this book had approached your girlfriend while you were at work? You'd want your girlfriend to do the right thing and be truthful wouldn't you!

These truthful kinds of girls are exactly the kind of girls all guys want, so if she was to do the dirty on her boyfriend then she'd no longer be that truthful kind of girl would she!

When this happens to me, I tend to just thank her for her time and say how lucky the chap must be to be dating the kind of girl who wouldn't cheat on him. I've been known to add them on Facebook, because hey, you never know they may end up breaking up a few weeks or months down the line. Always be respectful!

Question: Damn iPhones, I stopped this girl and she's adding me on Facebook but my profile is a mess, this is really going to ruin my chances! What can I do?

Well I recognise that Facebook is not only the future but it's the present as well. Make sure your profile is not a mess. In fact if you get as far as an ID with any girl it's inevitable she's going to want to add you! In fact I'm guessing you want to do the same right?

I've written a whole book on Facebook pick up, it's actually quite a big subject in itself. But make sure you clean your profile up for any new girls you add. Delete any photos that paint you in a bad light. No topless photos of you posing in the mirror for heavens sake. No photos of you taking a picture of yourself with an outstretched arm, you know the ones I mean. Delete any wall posts that make you look boring or mundane. Don't make it look like you spend your life on Facebook either.

She's going to go over your profile with a fine toothed comb and no doubt you'll do the same to her, so keep all these things in your mind. I've had girls go back three years into my history to find things out about me.

Question: What about kino escalation?

Kino escalation is always a good idea and I recommend you begin right from your introduction with a handshake. From there you should try and get in little touches wherever possible but only when it makes sense to do it. It's easy to give a tap on the girls elbow when you're emphasising a point!

I always recommend giving the girl a kiss on both cheeks when you say your goodbyes!

Question: Should I try peacocking for day game?

Erm, not really! I would just dress as yourself and don't try to be anything you're not. Wearing silly hats to make you stand out in the street is just a little weird for me.

I did though discover a nice little tip quite by accident while I was working in Manchester, England. Some girl was handing out free miniature potted plants along with business cards to try and promote her flower business. She ended up giving me three free potted plants. I had a long walk from where I was working to my car and I was so amazed by the amount of glances I got from women I decided to buy some the next day and begin the trip again with the intention of doing some day game.

Seriously, if you want to "peacock" or even get some super easy PAP's get yourself some tiny plant pots and plant yourself some cute little daisy looking flowers. Or buy some, it's up to you.

I even experimented with different amounts of plants to carry around with me. Carrying one doesn't seem to have the same effect for some reason. I think three really is the magic number, it draws lots of attention. When you're speaking to the girls you can even have fun handing her one of the plants so you can shake her other hand. You can even give her one of the plants as a gift! Tell her to look after it! There's no way you're not going to stand out following this! You'll have things to discuss on your date too such as how well is she looking after your favourite plant! I will mention that Neil Strauss in his book The Game mentions that he gives girls bracelets, trinkets or necklaces and he asks the girl to look after it until they meet up on their first date. I can only imagine doing that with a living plant would be even more powerful.

Question: Is going direct really the best method for day game? I've read other PUA's recommend only going indirect!

Well it's all a matter of opinion really. Sure, many PUA's really will prefer indirect to direct, even in the day time, although I personally have never found it to work anywhere near as well as direct for the day time.

They are of course welcome to their opinion as I am welcome to mine. But it seems that more and more PUA's are coming round to the idea of direct when it comes to day game.

Question: I read that if you walk up to a girl and tell her she's stunning then you're giving away all your power because she knows she already has you without having to do anything! What do you have to say about this Charlie?

Well firstly, the way you've phrased your question makes it sound like you've not as of yet even tried the direct approach, so how will you know if it will work or not? Sure there may be some women out there who will be put off by the direct approach, but to be honest I haven't really met many at all. The advantages of DDG far outweigh any disadvantages such as giving away any power to the girl you've just told is stunning. But I've thought about all this for you. This is why I always add into my approaches, "I really hope you're friendly too!" This way you're taking the power back, you're demonstrating that while yes she may well be stunning, you still haven't made your mind up about her. By dropping that little extra bit into the opener you're showing her that she still has to work for you because it takes more than just her looks to totally win you over.

Question: So you've been doing this a while huh? You must have some pretty funny stories?

I did one time approach a girl who I'd worked with a couple of years earlier, I just didn't recognise her. You've just got to grind on when that happens. It only got embarrassing when I ended up working with her again 6 months afterwards in a different job.

My former instructor did have plenty of funny stories. He used to go round day gaming so often in London that he'd ended up approaching the same girl twice within the same month using the same line. His approach was indirect and I don't think it had the same effect. The lesson from the story was that he never let the fact she recognised him from earlier that month effect his game. He just carried on with the pick up as if she'd never said anything.

The unexpected will happen when you start making lots of approaches. The key is to not let anything affect you. Confident guys do not let things out of their control dictate their feelings or emotions. When you start doing plenty of approaches, you will find you remember the good ones and forget the bad. You will also improve your life because you'll be making friends along the way too.

Question: I'm suffering from extreme approach anxiety! Sometimes I walk around for hours and I pass up so many opportunities to speak to girls, I just always cop out. What can I do?

Hey, I feel for you, I've been there! I probably had approach anxiety even worse than you did. I'm assuming you've been learning quite a bit of material and you have so much crap going through your mind. As I state in my other book Destroy Approach Anxiety, the key is to forget everything you know and go back to basics. The basics are what you've read in this book! Keep it simple! Remember how I said I actually had more guts approaching girls before I started reading all this material. AA only comes through filling your head with all these techniques trying to become the perfect PUA before you've even made a single approach. It's an impossible feat to achieve!

Make a commitment to yourself! Invest in this! Do what I did, go to a strange city, hire an instructor, pay your money, stay in a nice hotel and promise yourself you'll treat yourself to the best meal of your life if you can make twenty approaches over the course of one or two days. If you spend money doing all this stuff your brain will force you to make the most of it. Trust me!

Question: What other PAP signals have you got under your belt?

The best ones tend to be spontaneous, there really is an endless amount and it all depends on your situation. If you're reading a book in the coffee shop you can pretend to be bored and fall asleep. You can point to her, to yourself and then make the gesture for eating a meal. For the gym you can flex a muscle or bench press thin air. There is always the universal sticking out of tongue that can be used anywhere! The wave is also universal! It only gets a little tricky when you're in the street because you're both moving. This is why eye contact and a nice friendly smile or hello should never be underestimated.

Conclusion

Well that's it! I've made it as simple as I possibly can because it really should be that simple!

So now I want you to promise me one thing! Do not buy any more pick up books, read any more forum posts or watch any more Youtube approach videos until you've made at least ten approaches.

You really do need to complete level one in the field before you try to skip to level ten in your head.

I understand that many guys reading this will be nervous as hell about approaching beautiful women in the street and telling them how stunning they are. But believe me, it really does get easier and if you can do that then you can do anything, it will improve your life in ways you can't imagine!

I'm sure you know that feeling of seeing a beautiful girl you wished you knew how to talk to and watching her walk out of your life forever. Well don't let that happen to you ever again!

You really do have all the info you need right in this book, so please don't complicate things any more by filling your head with methods from other books. There is no magic bullet that will make things easier for you. When it's all said and done, you're going to have to take the bull by the horns and start approaching women.

If you've enjoyed this book and feel that others may benefit from it too then why not leave an honest review on the sales page. Many thanks for reading and I wish you the best of luck in the world.

Also by Charlie Valentino

First Date Tips for Men

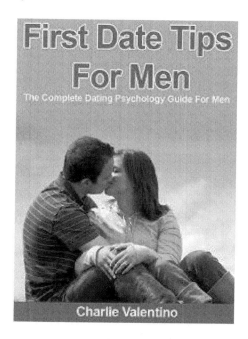

The complete dating psychology guide for men! - This powerful book gives men the ability to completely captivate women on dates.

There are many techniques and strategies in First Date Tips for Men, some practical, others logistical. However it is the psychological tips, the getting into the female mind, to have her thinking about you even after the date is over that really makes this book truly unique.

Here's a few of the things you'll learn inside:

- How to compliment her correctly to get her to open up to you.
- Establishing a connection. This will make her feel like she's known you a long time.
- Rapport breaking. This is powerful and will make her chase you.
- Qualification. This is the secret weapon. Few guys use qualification! This is how you stand out and get her to chase you for a long time.

If only I knew these things as a teenager!

Meet Women on Facebook

by: charlie valentino

Meeting women on Facebook is easy, as long as you know what you're doing!

You need a profile that makes you stand out from the rest of the guys out there, who message random girls all the time hoping for a response.

Learn how to craft the best Facebook profile possible to enable picking up girls on Facebook easy!

After that, use our Facebook pick up lines to pique her interest and have her impatiently message you back.

It's all here in Meet Women on Facebook to make Facebook pick up easy for any guy out there.

No matter if she's an existing Facebook friend, a friend of a friend or you have no connection with her whatsoever, discover the complete formula from the first message to the first date now.

With most of the world's hot girls on Facebook, Facebook dating is the future! Don't miss the boat on this one!

Destroy Approach Anxiety – Effortlessly Approach Women without Fear

Approach anxiety is something the vast majority of aspiring pick up artists suffer from when starting out approaching girls. If we can't get over approach anxiety, our first major stumbling block in the world of pick up then we're not going to meet many attractive women.

Destroy Approach Anxiety covers this subject so you can get over this easily and then on to the good stuff which is approaching women without fear.

Find out the true reasons why we suffer from approach anxiety, it may surprise you. One of the author's beliefs is that it's the overloading of information in our heads in an attempt to gain perfection before we've even made our first approach. This is impossible!

The author emphasizes the importance of keeping pick up as simple as possible, especially when suffering from approach anxiety. He gives numerous strategies for maintaining the perfect pick up, without overloading the head with too much information, which you can't possibly act on when under pressure approaching hot women.

Destroy Approach Anxiety should be the first PUA book you read as it will help you find approaching girls in the street as simple as possible by getting you in the right frame of mind.

Confidence for Men

24 Instant Confidence Boosting Tips

by: charlie valentino

This revolutionary book which aims to help men from all walks of life improve their self-confidence contains 24 chapters of easy to implement tips and strategies.

Discover the subtle body language traits which all confident men have and how you can use confident body language to actually fool your brain into thinking you're a confident man.

Learn about becoming a leader, one of the most important things all confident people have in common.

You'll also find out how to create the best possible social circle, the importance of identifying and cutting out negative people who bring you down and instead finding and including those people who'll add to your life.

Building self-confidence to last you the rest of your life begins with taking action! Confidence for Men emphasizes the importance of taking action. That action starts here!

Online Dating For Men

Online Dating
For Men

Charlie Valentino

1 in 5 new relationships now begin from an online dating site. Given that only a few short years ago this figure was zero, this is quite impressive. It is estimated that within a few years, the vast majority of new relationships will begin through meeting on an online dating site!

Having said that, 95% of all men who sign up to an internet dating site will give up within one subscription term.

Charlie Valentino has now authored his sixth relationship book for men, aiming to help guys meet their dream girl whether on Match.com, Plenty of Fish or any other online dating site.

In this book you'll learn:

- The mind set and strategy you must take to set yourself apart from all the other guys online.

- The pitfalls of online dating and why most men fail.

- The webs best online dating sites and which ones to avoid.

- All you need to know to create the single best profile that will stop women in their tracks. Crafting that perfect profile is the single most important thing you must do to ensure women return your emails. Charlie Valentino previously authored Meet Women on Facebook and is an expert on creating enticing online profiles.

- Discover the many mistakes that men make with their profiles so you can ensure you don't make the same mistakes.

- Learn how to craft the perfect opening email to send to girls to give yourself the highest possible chance of receiving a reply.

- Charlie also shows you his tried and tested cut and paste email system.

- See evidence of what 99% of guys are doing and why it's impossible for them to stand out and make any impact. This is valuable information to know, so you don't do the same.

Online Dating For Men contains all you need to know in order to attract women online, improving dramatically your chances of dating as many women as you like through online dating websites.

The Alpha Male System

The Alpha Male System

8 Elements To Becoming
Alpha Male!

Charlie Valentino

The Alpha Male System concentrates on eight fundamental alpha male elements which are visible as well as desirable in all leaders of men, which women also happen to crave in abundance.

In the days of the "metro sexual," men with alpha male traits and qualities are becoming rarer and increasingly more sought after.

Those few alpha males who can lead people, command respect and change the dynamic of a room simply by walking in it have all the luck. Or is it luck?

Discover the eight alpha male elements which will change your life along with detailed plans to attain them.

Becoming an alpha male is possible for most people, as long as you're willing to put a little work into yourself.

Made in the USA
Lexington, KY
10 October 2014